Book of My Nights

Book of My Nights

Poems by

Li-Young Lee

David,

Night is vast,
the stars countless,
where's home?

Peace,

AMERICAN POETS CONTINUUM SERIES, NO. 68

BOA Editions, Ltd. ❦ Rochester, New York. ❦ 2001

02 03 7 6 5 4 3

Publications by BOA Editions, Ltd. — a not-for-profit corporation under section 501 (c) (3) of the United States Internal Revenue Code — are made possible with the assistance of grants from the Literature Program of the New York State Council on the Arts, the Literature Program of the National Endowment for the Arts, the Sonia Raiziss Giop Charitable Foundation, The Halcyon Hill Foundation, The Chase Manhattan Foundation, as well as from the Mary S. Mulligan Charitable Trust, the County of Monroe, NY, and The CIRE Foundation. See page 66 for special individual acknowledgments.

Cover Design: Daphne Poulin-Stofer.
Art: *Ambiguity's Child,* Stephen Carpenter, courtesy of the artist.
Interior design and composition: Valerie Brewster, Scribe Typography
Manufacturing: McNaughton & Gunn, Lithographers
BOA Logo: Mirko

LIBRARY OF CONGRESS CATALOGING-IN-PUBLICATION DATA

Lee, Li-Young, 1957–
Book of my nights: poems / by Li-Young Lee.
    p. cm. — (American poets continuum series; no 68)
ISBN 1-929918-07-0 (alk. paper) — ISBN 1-929918-08-9 (pbk: alk. paper)
    I. Asian Americans — Poetry. I. Title. II. American poets continuum series; vol. 68.
PS3562.E35438 B66 2001
811'.54 — DC21   2001037760

BOA Editions, Ltd.
Steven Huff, Publisher
Richard Garth, Chair, Board of Directors
A. Poulin, Jr., President & Founder (1976–1996)
260 East Avenue, Rochester, NY 14604

www.boaeditions.org

NYSCA

NATIONAL
ENDOWMENT
FOR THE ARTS

For Donna

your voice
the lasting echo
of my heart's calling
me home

Contents

Book of My Nights

Pillow

There's nothing I can't find under there.
Voices in the trees, the missing pages
of the sea.

Everything but sleep.

And night is a river bridging
the speaking and the listening banks,

a fortress, undefended and inviolate.

There's nothing that won't fit under it:
fountains clogged with mud and leaves,
the houses of my childhood.

And night begins when my mother's fingers
let go of the thread
they've been tying and untying
to touch toward our fraying story's hem.

Night is the shadow of my father's hands
setting the clock for resurrection.

Or is it the clock unraveled, the numbers flown?

There's nothing that hasn't found home there:
discarded wings, lost shoes, a broken alphabet.

Everything but sleep. And night begins

with the first beheading
of the jasmine, its captive fragrance
rid at last of burial clothes.

A Table in the Wilderness

I draw a window
and a man sitting inside it.

I draw a bird in flight above the lintel.

That's my picture of *thinking*.

If I put a woman there instead
of the man, it's a picture of *speaking*.

If I draw a second bird
in the woman's lap, it's *ministering*.

A third flying below her feet.
Now it's *singing*.

Or erase the birds,
make ivy branching
around the woman's ankles, clinging
to her knees, and it becomes *remembering*.

You'll have to find your own
pictures, whoever you are,
whatever your need.

As for me, many small hands
issuing from a waterfall
means silence
mothered me.

The hours hung like fruit in night's tree
means when I close my eyes
and look inside me,

a thousand open eyes
span the moment of my waking.

Meanwhile, the clock
adding a grain to a grain
and not getting bigger,

subtracting a day from a day
and never having less, means the honey

lies awake all night
inside the honeycomb
wondering who its parents are.

And even my death isn't my death
unless it's the unfathomed brow
of a nameless face.

Even my name isn't my name
except the bees assemble

a table to grant a stranger
light and moment in a wilderness
of *Who? Where?*

From Another Room

Who lay down at evening
and woke at night
a stranger to himself? A country

wholly unfound to himself, who wondered
behind closed eyes
if his fate meant winter knitting

outcome underground, summer
overdue, or spring's pure parable, the turning
in every turning thing, fruit and flower,
jar, spindle, and story?

He's the one who heard
the hidden dove's troubled voice
and has been asking
ever since: Whose sleep
builds and unbuilds those great rooms, Night and Day?

He's the one who knows
what a gleaned thing his own voice is,
something the birds
discarded, trading for a future. Call him

one whom night found beyond
the fallen gate,

where the mower never mows,
with no way to go but toward
the growing shadow of the earth.

Call him the call embarked
in search of itself, a black dew receding
unto its own beginnings.

Depending on who you ask,
his mother or his night, he's either
the offspring of his childhood or his death.

Depending on who his mother is in his dreams—
beggar, thief, boatman, mist—

he's either a man paused
on the stairs, thinking he heard
the names he used as a boy
behind his parents' house,
during evening games of lost and found,

or else a child
reading out loud to himself
from his favorite book every morning.

One day, he finds his own voice
strange, himself no longer
the names his playmates knew him by,
but not yet the boundless
quiet of his mother's watching
from another room.

Nativity

In the dark, a child might ask, *What is the world?*
just to hear his sister
promise, *An unfinished wing of heaven,*
just to hear his brother say,
A house inside a house,
but most of all to hear his mother answer,
One more song, then you go to sleep.

How could anyone in that bed guess
the question finds its beginning
in the answer long growing
inside the one who asked, that restless boy,
the night's darling?

Later, a man lying awake,
he might ask it again,
just to hear the silence
charge him, *This night*
arching over your sleepless wondering,

this night, the near ground
every reaching-out-to overreaches,

just to remind himself
out of what little earth and duration,
out of what immense good-bye,

each must make a safe place of his heart,
before so strange and wild a guest
as God approaches.

Hurry toward Beginning

Is it because the hour is late
the dove sounds new,

no longer asking
a path to its father's house,
no longer begging shoes of its mother?

Or is it because I can't tell departure
from arrival, the host from the guest,

the one who waits expectant at the window
from the one who, even now, tramples the dew?

I can't tell what my father said about the sea
we crossed together
from the sea itself,

or the rose's noon from my mother
crying on the stairs, lost
between a country and a country.

Everywhere is home to the rain.
The hours themselves, where do they hide?
The fruit of listening, what's that?

Are days the offspring of distracted hands?
Does waiting that grows out of waiting
grow lighter? What does my death weigh?
What's earlier, thirst or shade?
Is all light late, the echo to some prior bell?

Is it because I'm tired that I don't know?
Or is it because I'm dying?
When will I be born? Am I the flower,
wide awake inside the falling fruit?
Or a man waiting for a woman
asleep behind a door?
What if a word unlocks
room after room the days
wait inside? Still,

night amasses a foreground
current to my window.
Listen. Whose footsteps are those
hurrying toward beginning?

Little Round

My fool asks: Do the years spell a path to later
be remembered? Who's there to read them back?

My death says: One bird knows the hour and suffers
to house its millstone-weight as song.

My night watchman lies down
in a room by the sea
and hears the water telling,
out of a thousand mouths,
the story behind his mother's sleeping face.

My eternity shrugs and yawns:
Let the stars knit and fold
inside their numbered rooms. When night asks
who I am I answer, *Your own,* and am not lonely.

My loneliness, my sleepless darling
reminds herself
the fruit that falls increases
at the speed of the body rising to meet it.

And my child? He sleeps and sleeps.

And my mother? She divides
the rice, today's portion from tomorrow's,
tomorrow's from ever after.

And my father. He faces me and rows
toward what he can't see.

And my God.
What have I done with my God?

Black Petal

I never claimed night fathered me.
That was my dead brother talking in his sleep.
I keep him under my pillow, a dear wish
that colors my laughing and crying.

I never said the wind, remembering nothing,
leaves so many rooms unaccounted for,
continual farewell must ransom
the unmistakable fragrance
our human days afford.

It was my brother, little candle in the pulpit,
reading out loud to all of earth
from the book of night.

He died too young to learn his name.
Now he answers to Vacant Boat,
Burning Wing, My Black Petal.

Ask him who his mother is. He'll declare the birds
have eaten the path home, but each of us
joins night's ongoing story
wherever night overtakes him,
the heart astonished to find belonging
and thanks answering thanks.

Ask if he's hungry or thirsty,
he'll say he's the bread come to pass
and draw you a map
to the twelve secret hips of honey.

Does someone want to know the way to spring?
He'll remind you
the flower was never meant to survive
the fruit's triumph.

He says an apple's most secret cargo
is the enduring odor of a human childhood,
our mother's linen pressed and stored, our father's voice
walking through the rooms.

He says he's forgiven our sister
for playing dead and making him cry
those afternoons we were left alone in the house.

And when clocks frighten me with their long hair,
and when I spy the wind's numerous hands
in the orchard unfastening
first the petals from the buds,
then the perfume from the flesh,

my dead brother ministers to me. His voice
weighs nothing
but the far years between
stars in their massive dying,

and I grow quiet hearing
how many of both of our tomorrows
lie waiting inside it to be born.

The Well

As for the lily, who knows
if what we face isn't the laughter

of one who went while the time seemed green
for going, or a voice

one room ahead of our own dreaming, and we die
at the crest of each day's spending

away. As prow and the surrendered foam
go on forgetting, our very looking is the light

feasting on the light. As for hunger,
each must cross to a body as yet unnamed.

Who needs a heart unless it's one we share
with a many-windowed sea? A heart,

and not the dark it moves through, not the waves
it births, but, visited by blood, unoccupied,

is the very wheel installing day, the well
from which paired hands set out, happy
to undress a terrifying and abundant yes.

Night Mirror

Li-Young, don't feel lonely
when you look up
into great night and find
yourself the far face peering
hugely out from between
a star and a star. All that space
the nighthawk plunges through,
homing, all that distance beyond embrace,
what is it but your own infinity.

And don't be afraid
when, eyes closed, you look inside you
and find night is both
the silence tolling after stars
and the final word
that founds all beginning, find night,

abyss and shuttle,
a finished cloth
frayed by the years, then gathered
in the songs and games
mothers teach their children.

Look again
and find yourself changed
and changing, now the bewildered honey

fallen into your own hands,
now the immaculate fruit born of hunger.
Now the unequaled perfume of your dying.
And time? Time is the salty wake
of your stunned entrance upon
no name.

Heir to All

What I spill in a dream
runs under my door,
ahead of my arrival
and the year's wide round,

to meet me in the color of hills
at dawn, or else collected
in a flower's name
I trace with my finger
in a book. Proving

only this: Listening is the ground
below my sleep,
where decision is born, and

whoever's heard the title
autumn knows him by
is heir to all those
unfurnished rooms inside the roses.

Discrepancies, Happy and Sad

We've moved into a bigger house.
Now our voices wander among the rooms
calling, *Where are you?*

And what we can't forget
of other houses confuses us
as we answer back and forth, *Over here!*

It's a little like returning to the village
where you were born, the sad bewilderment
of discrepancies between
what you remember and what's there.

No. It's more like a memory of heaven.
Voices coming closer, voices moving away,

and what we thought we knew
about life on earth confounding us.

And then that question
from which all the other questions begin.

My Father's House

Here, as in childhood, Brother, no one sees us.
And someone has died, and someone is not yet born.

Our father walks through his church at night
and sets all the clocks for spring. His sleeplessness

weighs heavy on my forehead, his death almost
nothing. In the letter he never wrote to us

he says, *No one can tell how long it takes a seed*
to declare what death and lightning told it

while it slept. But stand at a window long enough,
late enough, and you may some night hear

a secret you'll tomorrow, parallel to the morning,
tell on a wide, white bed, to a woman

like a sown ledge of wheat. Or you may never
tell it, who lean across the night and miles of the sea,

to arrive at a seed, in whose lamplit house
resides a thorn, or a wee man carving

a name on a stone, the name of the one who has died,
the name of the one not born unknown.

Someone has died. Someone is not yet born.
And during this black interval,

I sweep all three floors of our father's house,
and I don't count the broom strokes; I row

up and down for nothing but love: his for me, my own
for the threshold, and for the woman's voice

I hear while I sweep, as though she swept beside me,
a woman whose face, if she owns a face at all,

is its own changing. And if I know her name
I know to say it so softly she need not

stop her work to hear me. Though when she lies down
at night, in the room of our arrival,

she'll know I called her.
And when she answers it's morning,

which even now is overwhelming, the woman
combing her hair opposite to my departure.

And only now and then do I lean at a jamb
to see if I can see what I thought I heard.

I heard her ask, *My love, why can't you sleep?*
and answer, *Someone has died, and someone*

is not yet born. Meanwhile, I hear the voices
of women telling a story in the round,

and I sit down on the rough stoop, by the sea grass,
and go on folding the laundry I was folding,

the everyday clothes of our everyday life, the death
clothes wearing us clean to the bone.

And I know the tide is rising early,
and I can't hope to trap the story

told in the round. But the woman I know
says, *Sleep,* so I lie down on the clothes,

the folded and unfolded, the life and the death.
Ages go by. When I wake, the story has changed

the firmament into domain, domain
into a house, and the sun speaks the day,

unnaming, showing the telling, dissipating
the boundaries of the story to include

the one who has died and the one not yet born.
How still the morning grows about the voice

of one child reading to another.
How much a house is house at all due

to one room where an elder child reads
to his brother. And the younger knows by heart

the brother-voice. How dark the other rooms,
how slow morning comes

collected in a name
told at one sill

and listened for at the threshold of dew.
What book is this we read

together, Brother, and at which window
of our father's house? In which upper room?

We read it twice: once in two voices, to each other,
and once in unison, to children

and the sun, our star, that vast office
we sit inside while birds lend their church

sown in air, realized in a body uttering
windows, growing rafters, couching seeds.

The Moon from Any Window

The moon from any window is one part
whoever's looking.

The part I can't see
is everything my sister keeps to herself.

One part my dead brother's sleepless brow,

the other part the time I waste, the time
I won't have.

But which is the lion
killed for the sake of the honey inside him,

and which the wine, stranded
in a valley, unredeemed?

And don't forget the curtains. Don't forget the wind
in the trees, or my mother's voice saying things
that will take my whole life to come true.

One part earnest child grown tall
in his mother's doorway, and one a last look
over the shoulder before leaving.

And never forget it answers to no address,
but calls wave after wave
to a path of thirst. Never forget

the candle climbing down
without glancing back.

And what about the heart
counting alone, out loud, in that game
in which the many hide from the one?

Never forget the cry
completely hollowed of the dying one
who cried it.

Only in such pure outpouring
is there room for all this night.

Degrees of Blue

At the place in the story

where a knock at the hull wakes the dreamer
and he opens his eyes to find the rowers gone,
the boat tied to an empty dock,

the boy looks up from his book,

out the window, and sees
the hills have turned their backs,
they are walking into evening.

How long does he watch them go?
Does the part of him that follows
call for years across his growing sadness?

When he returns to the tale,
the page is dark,

and the leaves at the window have been traveling
beside his silent reading
as long as he can remember.

Where is his father?
When will his mother be home?

How is he going to explain
the moon taken hostage, the sea
risen to fill up all the mirrors?

How is he going to explain the branches
beginning to grow from his ribs and throat,
the cries and trills starting in his own mouth?

And now that ancient sorrow between his hips,
his body's ripe listening
the planet
knowing itself at last.

The Sleepless

Like any ready fruit, I woke
falling toward beginning and

welcome, all of night
the only safe place.

Spoken for, I knew
a near hand would meet me
everywhere I heard my name

and the stillness ripening
around it. I found my inborn minutes
decreed, my death appointed
and appointing. And singing
collects the earth

about my rest,
making of my heart
the way home.

Our River Now

Say night is a house you inherit,
and in the room in which you hear the sea
declare its countless and successive deaths,
tolling the dimensions of your dying,

you close your eyes and dream
the king's bees build the king's honey
in the furthest reaches of your childhood.
Wouldn't you set your clocks
by that harvest?

And didn't you, a sleepless child
saying to yourself the name
your parents gave you over and over,
hear both the ringing sum of you
such sound accounted for
and all the rest, the dumb
throng of you, that never answered to a word,

that stands even now assembled where
your calling brinks, the unutterable
luring your voice out of its place of rocks
and into a multitude of waters?
But what was it I meant to say?

Something about our beginningless past.
Maybe. Maybe our river, dreaming out loud,
folds story and forgetting.

The Bridge

The stars report a vast consequence
our human moment joins.

Or is it all the dark
around them speaking?

And if someone who listened for years
one night hears *Home,*

what is he to do with the story
his bones hum to him
about the dust?

Let him go in search of the hiding place
of the dew, where the hours are born.

Let him uncover whose heart
beats behind the falling leaves.

And as for the one who hears *Remember,*

well, I began to sing
the words my father sang
when he knelt to teach me
how to tie my shoes:

Crossing over, crossing under, little bird,
build your bridge by nightfall.

Words for Worry

Another word for *father* is *worry.*

Worry boils the water
for tea in the middle of the night.

Worry trimmed the child's nails before
singing him to sleep.

Another word for *son* is *delight,*
another word, *hidden.*

And another is *One-Who-Goes-Away.*
Yet another, *One-Who-Returns.*

So many words for son:
He-Dreams-for-All-Our-Sakes.
His-Play-Vouchsafes-Our-Winter-Share.
His-Dispersal-Wins-the-Birds.

But only one word for *father.*
And sometimes a man is both.
Which is to say sometimes a man
manifests mysteries beyond
his own understanding.

For instance, being the one and the many,
and the loneliness of either. Or

the living light we see by, we never see. Or

the sole word weighs
heavy as a various name.

And sleepless worry folds the laundry for tomorrow.
Tired worry wakes the child for school.

Orphan worry writes the note he hides
in the child's lunch bag.
It begins, *Dear Firefly....*

Little Father

I buried my father
in the sky.
Since then, the birds
clean and comb him every morning
and pull the blanket up to his chin
every night.

I buried my father underground.
Since then, my ladders
only climb down,
and all the earth has become a house
whose rooms are the hours, whose doors
stand open at evening, receiving
guest after guest.
Sometimes I see past them
to the tables spread for a wedding feast.

I buried my father in my heart.
Now he grows in me, my strange son,
my little root who won't drink milk,
little pale foot sunk in unheard-of night,
little clock spring newly wet
in the fire, little grape, parent to the future
wine, a son the fruit of his own son,
little father I ransom with my life.

Lullaby

After crying, Child,
there's still singing to be done.

Your voice, the size of the heart's
first abandonment,
is for naming

the span each falling thing endures,
and then for sounding
a country under speech, dark hillsides

of an older patience outwaiting
what you or your mother and father
could ever say.

What does day proclaim there
where birds glean all of our
remaindered sleep? After wings

and the shadows of wings, there's still
the whole ungrasped body
of flying to uncover.

After standing, outnumbered, under petals
and their traceless falling
out of yesterday
into open want,

we're still the fruit to meet,
still the ancient shapes
of jars and bowls to weigh,

and still the empty hands
in which the hours never pool.

One Heart

Look at the birds. Even flying
is born

out of nothing. The first sky
is inside you, open

at either end of day.
The work of wings

was always freedom, fastening
one heart to every falling thing.

Praise Them

The birds don't alter space.
They reveal it. The sky
never fills with any
leftover flying. They leave
nothing to trace. It is our own
astonishment collects
in chill air. Be glad.
They equal their due
moment never begging,
and enter ours
without parting day. See
how three birds in a winter tree
make the tree barer.
Two fly away, and new rooms
open in December.
Give up what you guessed
about a whirring heart, the little
beaks and claws, their constant hunger.
We're the nervous ones.
If even one of our violent number
could be gentle
long enough that one of them
found it safe inside
our finally untroubled and untroubling gaze,
who wouldn't hear
what singing completes us?

Build by Flying

I lean on a song.
I follow a story.
I keep my mother waiting
when she asks, *How long*
before the wren finishes the grain?
How soon until we see
what a house the birds
build by flying? In the dream
in which I stopped with her
under branches, on the long way home from school,
one of us, curious
about the fruit overhead, asked:
To what port has the fragrance so lately
embarked, for whose tables?
One of us waited for the answer.
And one went on alone,
singing. And all the place
there was grew out of listening.

In the Beginning

A woman is speaking in a place of rocks.

Her voice is the water of that place
and founds the time there.

She says the world, begun out of nothing,
stands by turning

out of grasp, a lover's *yes* and *no,*
stay and go, singing stepping
in and out of time and momentum,

the body's doctrine
of need and scarcity,

the heart's full measure
of night and day, sons and daughters.

A woman is talking. Her voice
is a boat and oars in a place of rocks.

Stranded in a rocky place,
it is a garment torn to pieces.

It is the light,
accomplished by wind and fire,
abiding inside the rocks.

A memory of the sea, it's what remains.
Homesickness in the rocks.
Homecoming in the trees.

The Other Hours

When I look at the ocean, I see
a house in various stages of ruin and beginning.

When I listen to the wind in the trees,
I hear—or is it someone inside me hears—
the far voice of a woman reading out loud
from a book that opens everywhere onto day.

Her voice makes a place, and the birds
go there carrying nothing but the sky.

When I think about the hills where I was born,
someone—is he inside me? Beside me?
Does he have a mother or father, brother or sister?

Is he my dismembered story
fed to the unvanquished roses?

Is he the rosebud packed in sleep and fire,
counted, tendered, herded toward the meeting foretold?

Which of us is awake tonight?
Which of us is the lamp? Which the shadow?

Someone who won't answer remembers laughter
that sires the rocks and trees,

that fetches in its ancient skirts
the fateful fruits and seeds.

The Hammock

When I lay my head in my mother's lap
I think how day hides the stars,
the way I lay hidden once, waiting
inside my mother's singing to herself. And I remember
how she carried me on her back
between home and the kindergarten,
once each morning and once each afternoon.

I don't know what my mother's thinking.

When my son lays his head in my lap, I wonder:
Do his father's kisses keep his father's worries
from becoming his? I think, *Dear God,* and remember
there are stars we haven't heard from yet:
They have so far to arrive. *Amen,*
I think, and I feel almost comforted.

I've no idea what my child is thinking.

Between two unknowns, I live my life.
Between my mother's hopes, older than I am
by coming before me, and my child's wishes, older than I am
by outliving me. And what's it like?
Is it a door, and good-bye on either side?
A window, and eternity on either side?
Yes, and a little singing between two great rests.

The Eternal Son

Someone's thinking about his mother tonight.

The wakeful son
of a parent who hardly sleeps,

the sleepless father of his own
restless child, God, is it you?
Is it me? Do you have a mother?

Who mixes flour and sugar
for your birthday cake?

Who stirs slumber and remembrance
in a song for your bedtime?

If you're the cry enjoining dawn,
who birthed you?

If you're the bell tolling night
without circumference, who rocked you?

Someone's separating
the white grains of his insomnia
from the black seeds
of his sleep.

If it isn't you, God, it must be me.

My mother's eternal son,
I can't hear the rain without thinking
it's her in the next room
folding our clothes to lay inside a suitcase.

And now she's counting her money
on the bed, the good paper
and the paper from the other country
in separate heaps.

If day comes soon, she could buy our passage.
But if our lot is the rest of the night,
we'll have to trust unseen hands
to hand us toward ever deeper sleep.

Then I'll be the crumb
at the bottom of her pocket,
and she can keep me
or sow me on the water,
as she pleases. Anyway,

she has too much to carry, she who knows
night must tell the rest of every story.

Now she's wondering about the sea.
She can't tell if the white foam laughs
I was born dark! while it spins
opposite the momentum of our dying,

or do the waves journey beyond
the name of every country
and the changing color of her hair.

And if she's weeping,
it's because she's misplaced
both of our childhoods.

And if she's humming, it's because
she's heard the name of life:
A name, but no name, the dove

bereft of memory and finally singing
how the light happened
to one who gave up
ever looking back.

A Dove! I Said

A dove! I said.

What I meant was all the colors
from ashes to singing.

What I meant was news
of my death,

a threshold
dividing my unmade tears
from the finished song.

Night, I said.
As in, *Night after night,*

as in, *Every night is two nights,*
a house under a hill. Night,

as in, *Night adds to night*
without remainder,

and all the nights are one
night, a book

whose every word is outcome,
whose every page is lifelong sentence.

What I meant was the wind
burying the dead.

What I should have said was:
A hand fallen still
at the foot of the burning hours,
paused between the written and the unwritten.

It was a mourning dove in my eaves.

And maybe I meant to say:
Child of time.

Maybe I should have called out:
Child of eternity.

Or did I only mean to ask, *Whose face*
did I glimpse last night in a dream?

Fill and Fall

As long as night is one country
on both sides of my window, I remain a face
dreaming a face

and trace the heart's steep path: Night
and falling.
There's no place

my hand, full of its own going away,
ever found along a body
falling beside me.

And the way to the crowning grapes lies sealed
to all but one who's heard
what nights are for: Falling,

as water falls
to fill and fall, overwhelming
basin after basin,

as each must kneel
inside himself to find
the tiered slopes
only brimming masters.

Dwelling

As though touching her
might make him known to himself,

as though his hand moving
over her body might find who
he is, as though he lay inside her, a country

his hand's traveling uncovered,
as though such a country arose
continually up out of her
to meet his hand's setting forth and setting forth.

And the places on her body have no names.
And she is what's immense about the night.
And their clothes on the floor are arranged
for forgetfulness.

Echo and Shadow

A room
and a room. And between them

she leans in the doorway
to say something,

lintel bright above her face,
threshold dark beneath her feet,

her hands behind her head gathering
her hair to tie and tuck at the nape.
A world and a world.

Dying and not dying.
And between them
the curtains blowing
and the shadows they make on her body,

a shadow of birds, a single flock,
a myriad body of wings and cries
turning and diving in complex unison.
Shadow of bells,

or the shadow of the sound
they make in the air, mornings, evenings,
everywhere I wait for her,

as even now her voice
seems a lasting echo
of my heart's calling me home, its story
an ocean beyond my human beginning,

each wave tolling the whole note
of my outcome and belonging.

Restless

I can hear in your voice
you were born in one country
and will die in another,

and where you live is where you'll be buried,
and when you dream it's where you were born,

and the moon never hangs in both skies
on the same night,

and that's why you think the moon has a sister,
that's why your day is hostage to your nights,

and that's why you can't sleep except by forgetting,
you can't love except by remembering.

And that's why you're divided: *yes* and *no*.
I want to die. I want to live.
Never go away. Leave me alone.

I can hear by what you say
your first words must have been *mother* and *father*.

Even before your own name, *mother*.
Long before *amen, father.*

And you put one word in your left shoe,
one in your right, and you go walking.

And when you lie down you tuck them
under your pillow, where they give rise
to other words: *childhood, fate,* and *rescue.*
Heaven, wine, return.

And even *god* and *death* are offspring.
Even *world* is begotten, even *summer*
a descendant. And the apple tree. Look and see

the entire lineage alive
in every leaf and branching
decision, snug inside each fast bud,

together in the flower, and again
in the pulp, mingling in the fragrance
of the first mouthful and the last.

I can tell by your silence you've seen the petals
immense in their vanishing.

Flying, they build your only dwelling.
Falling, they sow shadows at your feet.

And when you close your eyes
you can hear the ancient fountains
from which they derive,

rock and water ceaselessly declaring
the laws of coming and going.

Stations of the Sea

Regarding springtime, what is there to conclude?

One wing, I fall,
a third of the sum of flying.

Once forsaken, I remain
hidden in the dust, a mortal threshold
unearthed by crying.

Crying, my body turns to dark petals.

And of all the rooms in my childhood,
God was the largest
and most empty.

Of all my playmates,
my buried brother was the quietest,
never giving away my hiding place

where, my mother's Little-Know-Nothing,
I still await the dawning in my heart
of a name my mother and father never gave me,
my brothers and sisters never called me,

the name foretold
prior to my birth on any tree.

Among the roots, the dead
teem, memory of them
a storied amber risen
in my flesh.

Throughout the leaves, the wind,
unsurrounded, is reciting
the stations of the sea.

Buried Heart

The hyacinth emerges headlong dying,
one of the colors of ongoing
and good-bye,

its odor my very body's smokeless burning,

its voice
night's own dark lap.

Above ground, the crown of flowers tells the wish
brooding earth stitched inside the bulb.

In another kingdom, it was the wick
the lamp cradled, strands
assembled in rapt slumber.

Tonight it's a branching stair
the dead climb up to a hundred eyes enthroned,

and yet the hair I climb down
toward an earlier dream

and what I've always known:
Whoever lets the flowers fall
suffers his heart's withering
and growing scales,

whoever buries that horned root
inside himself becomes the ground

that sings, declaring a new circumference
even the stars enlarge by crowding down to hear.

Out of Hiding

Someone said my name in the garden,

while I grew smaller
in the spreading shadow of the peonies,

grew larger by my absence to another,
grew older among the ants, ancient

under the opening heads of the flowers,
new to myself, and stranger.

When I heard my name again, it sounded far,
like the name of the child next door,
or a favorite cousin visiting for the summer,

while the quiet seemed my true name,
a near and inaudible singing
born of hidden ground.

Quiet to quiet, I called back.
And the birds declared my whereabouts all morning.

Acknowledgments

My thanks go out to the editors of the following publications in whose pages several sections of this book have appeared: *The Best American Poetry of 1998, The Breadloaf Anthology of Comtemporary American Poetry, DoubleTake, The English Record, The Iron Horse Literary Review, The Kenyon Review, TriQuarterly, Water-Stone.*

I would like to express my sincerest gratitude to the Illinois Arts Council, the Lannan Foundation, and the National Endowment for the Arts for financial assistance that made the writing of these poems possible.

I am indebted to Ilya Kaminsky, Philip Levine, and Gerald Stern for suffering this book at various stages, to Thom Ward, editor at BOA Editions, for his close reading and untiring support of this work, and to Anthony Piccione for his relentless insistence on Being-in-the-Word. And to all of my family for keeping the circle whole.

About the Author

Li-Young Lee is the author of two previous books of poems, *Rose* (BOA Editions) and *The City in Which I Love You* (BOA Editions), and a book-length prose poem, *The Winged Seed* (Simon and Schuster, cloth; Ruminator Books, paperback). He has been the recipient of many literary awards, most recently The Lannan Foundation Literary Award, The American Book Award of the Before Columbus Foundation, and The PEN Oakland/Josephine Miles Award. He lives with his wife and two sons in Chicago, where he works in a warehouse.

BOA Editions, LTD.:
American Poets Continuum Series

COLOPHON

The publication of this book was made possible, in part, by the special support of the following individuals:

Pam & John Blanpied, Nancy & Alan Cameros
Sybil Craig, Dr. William & Shirley Ann Crosby
Peter & Suzanne Durant, Susan & Michael Feinstein
Dane & Judy Gordon, Richard Garth & Mimi Hwang
Deb & Kip Hale, Peter & Robin Hursh
Robert & Willy Hursh, Meg Kearney
Archie & Pat Kutz, Rosemary & Lew Lloyd
Peter & Phyllis Makuck, Suzanne D. Nelson
Kalliopy Paleos, Boo Poulin, Deborah Ronnen
Bernie & Jane Schuster, Pat & Michael Wilder
Geraldine Zetzel

* * *

Book of My Nights was set in Minion, with interior design and composition by Valerie Brewster, Scribe Typography, Port Townsend, WA.

The cover was designed by Daphne Poulin-Stofer.

The art, *Ambiguity's Child,* is by Stephen Carpenter, courtesy of the artist.

Manufacturing was by McNaughton & Gunn, Saline, MI.